MOSES AND THE PHARAOH

Written by
NOURA DURKEE
&
Illustrated by
AHMED JABIR

Copyright © Hood Hood Books, 1997

Hood Hood Books
46 Clabon Mews
London SW1X OEH

Tel; 44.171.5847878
Fax; 44.171.2250386
E-mail; info@hoodhood.co.uk
Website; www.hoodhood.co.uk

British Library Cataloguing-in-Publication Data
A catalogue record for this book is available from the British Library

ISBN 900251 27 2

No part of this book may be reproduced
in any form without prior permission from the publishers.
All rights reserved.

Origination by Fine Line Graphics, London
Printed by IPH, Egypt

PUBLISHER'S NOTE

Moses is not portrayed in the illustrations in this book. According to the *hadith* (saying) of the Prophet Muhammad (peace be upon him) it is traditional practice not to depict God's Angels, Messengers and Prophets in any form of visual representation.

Contents

English/Arabic Name Equivalents — iv

Introduction — v

Chapter 1 Lost and Found — 6

Chapter 2 In The Palace — 12

Chapter 3 A Terrible Night — 20

Chapter 4 The Desert — 29

Chapter 5 Back to Egypt — 36

Chapter 6 Trials — 45

Chapter 7 The Exodus — 52

ENGLISH/ARABIC NAME EQUIVALENTS

Aaron	Haroon
Abraham	Ibrahim
Isaac	Ishaq
Ishmael	Ismail
Joseph	Yusuf
Moses	Musa

Moses' sister, Qulthum, is called Miriam in the Old Testament (or the Jewish Bible), Book of Exodus and Numbers.

Moses' father-in-law, Shuayb, is called Jethro in the Old Testament, Book of Exodus.

Asiya is the name given to the Pharaoh's wife in the Quran. She plays the same part as the Pharaoh's daughter in the Old Testament, that is, finding the infant Moses floating on the river.

Haman, the Pharaoh's chief adviser in the Quran, is not the same as the Haman in the Old Testament (Book of Esther, Chapter 3 ff.). Haman in the Quran is probably an Arabicized version of Ha-Amen, the title given to every high priest of the Egyptian god, Amon.

The land of Madyan is spelt Midian in the Old Testament.

INTRODUCTION

Mainly based on Islamic tradition, Moses and the Pharaoh is a refreshing re-telling of this well-known story. It allows Western readers to appreciate Moses' life from a different perspective and Eastern readers to re-acquaint themselves with his miraculous story. The message of this book, as with all of the other titles in the LIVES OF THE PROPHETS series, is that of the tolerance and understanding that should exist among all peoples.

This book tells the first part of the story of the great Prophet, Moses. The main source is the Quran but some imaginary situations and conversations have been added to bring it alive for children. For example, some of the events in his childhood, and the conversations with his mother, brother and sister, are imaginary; they are based on knowledge of the life of Egypt at that time and the way he may have been raised in the palace of the Pharaoh. However, most of his talks with God and the Pharaoh reflect the account of the story in the Quran.

Moses is one of the most important prophets for Jews, Christians and Muslims. Like the story of Joseph, the story of Moses belongs to the Old Testament and the Quran, and fundamentally the story is much the same in all of them, although details such as the name of Moses' sister, Qulthum, in the Quran, is not mentioned in the Torah; and it is the Pharaoh's wife who finds the infant Moses on the river in the Quran whereas in the Bible it is his daughter. In general the Jewish tale has many more details – after all, the Jewish story is the history of a people as well as of a prophet.

Episodes from Moses' life feature many times in the Quran – but they are not described for the purposes of history; rather, Moses' story is used as an example for people of all time. It is used to point out many timeless truths such as courage, fear, faith, loneliness and power, and to show how one brave and holy man confronts the greatest tyrant on earth and, with the help of God, defeats him. It shows how God guides people if they both ask Him for help and help themselves as well. This is called hiero-history, sacred history – the history that goes beyond time and place because it is about the nature of all human beings and their relationship with God.

Moses' story is much longer than this book; after they all left Egypt many more things happened. Perhaps another time we shall continue the tale. For now, imagine yourself back about four thousand years or so on the banks of the River Nile....

Chapter 1
LOST AND FOUND

Qulthum crouched at the water's edge. There was a fly on her nose - she did not brush it off. Her feet were asleep - she did not move a muscle. She had worked for two or three years in the fields already; she knew the names of the great blue butterfly, the fat singing locust, the small green snake. She knew the calls of the water birds and the squishy sounds of the hippos rising out of the mud. She was only seven years old, but she knew how to keep still.

Right now she was so still that a tall ibis standing on one leg nearby didn't bother to move away, and a gull on its nest in the rushes was unruffled by her presence. A small fish flicked its tail on the calm surface of the water. The ibis' neck uncurled, its beak darted down, and the fish was caught, dripping in the air before being swallowed. The fly flew away from her nose. A frog croaked. Qulthum stayed still.

Through the green screen of water reeds she saw the basket bobbing and floating. It was a lovely basket; she and Mama had made it carefully out of these same reeds only the day before. They had woven it as tightly as they could and covered it with sap from the trees, and then with sticky black tar that they found bubbling up out of the ground. They had filled the inside with soft things, feathers and cotton and wool. "Just like making a bird's nest," laughed Qulthum to herself; and then came the sad moment of saying good-bye. Mama had fed the baby well so he would not cry. She and Mama helped each other not to cry too. "Be strong!" they had said to each other as they placed the sleeping baby lovingly in his basket bed.

And then in the early morning light they had carried the basket to the river and laid it bobbing in a quiet place beside the reeds. Mama had stayed a while, praying, and then gone home, instructing Qulthum to watch carefully and see what might happen.

Qulthum knew very well why Mama had chosen this particular spot. She herself had often watched here before. It was wonderful to see the ladies come down to the bank, to see them take off their golden crowns and bracelets and their jet-black wigs, to see them put their pretty painted toes in the water and to hear them giggle about how cold it was. Of course it wasn't cold at all. The mighty Nile could be cold sometimes, but this small quiet backwater was always warmed by the sun and protected by its walls of reeds. The royal ladies and their attendants used to play on the banks and some of them would get into the water in their white muslin dresses and splash about. They did not swim. Qulthum was sure that they did not know how, being royal ladies. She did.

But right now she wasn't thinking of swimming. She was watching the path that wound down to the water from the Pharaoh's palace. Someone was coming.

He was one of the palace guards. He had the arrogant walk of a man who knows that everyone will get out of his way, and he strode down the path with his arms swinging and his helmet shining in the morning light. He came to the water's edge, took a swift look around, and turned to go. At that instant Qulthum had to sneeze. She had to. Desperate, she put one hand over her nose and another over her mouth, and sank beneath the surface of the water. The sneeze, when it came, sounded like a cross between the croak of a bullfrog and the splash of a Nile fish. Qulthum, out of breath, could not stay down. Her head popped up and she looked fearfully towards the guard. He had turned in her direction and was listening carefully. There was no sound. Just then the ibis decided to take off, and lifted itself with a great flapping of wings into the blue air. Satisfied that the bird was the source of the sound, the guard strolled back up the hill. He had not even seen the basket.

Qulthum rubbed the mud off her dress, and sighed. She was shaking all over, and not from the cold. Those guards were ruthless with her people. Who knew what might happen if she was discovered spying on the Queen? And never mind her - what about the baby? They would kill him! But, thank heavens, he was still sleeping soundly. She prayed he would stay that way.

Soon after that she heard laughter on the path, and peeking carefully through the reeds, she saw the Pharaoh's wife and her attendants coming down to play. She stood stock-still. The ladies removed their ornaments and began to splash about in the water. The basket bobbed up and down in the ripples they made.

Released from the reeds, it floated a little way out into the pool, and one of the maids on the shore saw it. Calling to the others, she ran along the bank until she could just reach the basket with a long stick, and brought it in to land. Qulthum held her breath. What would they do?

The Queen, mildly interested, watched as the maids gathered in the basket, lifted it out of the water with exclamations of delight, and brought it over to her. She looked in. The baby chose that moment to open his eyes. He was three months old. He was plump and adorable. The Queen smiled and touched his cheek, and he smiled back. Thus began his career of winning the hearts and minds of people.

The Queen sat on the bank with the baby in her lap and wondered what to do. She wanted this baby. She loved him already. Yet he appeared to be one of the Children of Israel, the ones the Egyptians were forbidden to speak to. Her husband, the Pharaoh, said that they were worthless people, useful only to do all the hardest work in the land, making mud bricks, hoeing the earth, carrying heavy loads, cleaning

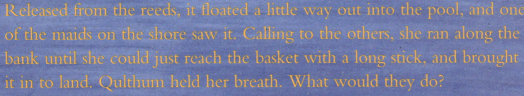

up after the superior Egyptians. Poor little thing. It was even said that a new law was to be enforced stating that all the boy babies of those people were to be killed at birth. "Oh dear," the Queen sighed, this must be a boy, and his mother must have kept him secretly and then left him to the blessings of the River Goddess, Hapi. She would help the goddess, she would look after him. He would be great fun to play with, and anyway, maybe her husband would adopt him as a son when he saw what a joy he was. He couldn't kill him! She knew how to touch the soft side of this Pharaoh. No one need know where the baby came from!

Just then the baby began to cry. The Queen tried to soothe him, but without success. She knew he must be hungry. There was an Egyptian wet nurse back at the palace. Quickly, for his cries were getting stronger, she rose to go. She handed the squalling baby to her favorite maid, lifted up her damp skirts, and began to walk up the path. The other ladies followed. The little basket boat was left bobbing by the shore.

Qulthum was in a quandary. Should she follow, and risk being seen? Should she go home and tell her mother? Mama already knew this was going to happen. God had told her in a dream not to worry as her baby would be well cared for. He had also told her that the baby would be returned to her. But how? Qulthum decided to follow. Squeezing the water out of her simple clothes, she crept along the edge of the reeds, trying to stay out of sight as long as possible while keeping the ladies in view. Then they disappeared through the back gate of the palace, and she knew that she would have to wait again. She went around to the front and squatted down with the beggars who always sat there. She waited for hours.

Inside, the ladies' quarters were in a turmoil. The Queen's new baby would not eat! One woman after another was brought to feed him, but each one was already nursing a baby, and the new one only screamed more loudly. Something had to be done! At last all the women of the palace had failed, and a maid ran to find someone from outside. Qulthum, waiting at the gate, recognized her and stood in her path. "Get out of my way, child, can't you see I'm in a hurry?" said the maid, none too politely. "The baby won't eat - such a fuss! He has a terrible temper!"

"Wait!" said Qulthum. "Would you like me to take you to a woman who will feed him? She's very good, I'm sure you won't be disappointed!"

"Wonderful," replied the maid, happy to have her work done for her. "If you can find me such a woman, I'll give you a present myself, and the Queen will pay her well!"

Off they went to Qulthum's mother, who was waiting at the door of her little house. Yes, she might take on a baby to nurse. Yes, she had a lot of milk and wouldn't mind coming to the palace - could her daughter come too? Yes, they might find some work for her to do about the place, but hurry, please hurry! So the conversation went, and so Moses' mother went happily to her baby, and he was given back to her to love and to feed; he was happy to eat, and the ladies were happy to have some peace again, and Qulthum was happy that it had all turned out so well. She and Mama visited the palace and took care of him from then on. The Queen named him Moses, and came to play with him whenever she felt like it. Otherwise they had him all to themselves. The two of them knew that God's promise had come true and they wondered what would happen next.

Chapter 2
IN THE PALACE

For a child, the palace of the Pharaoh contained a whole city of wonders. There were the columned halls with smooth shiny floors that you could run and slide on. There were the pools full of fat fish to feed. There were beautiful gardens with large-leafed plants to hide behind and flowers to put in your hair. There were the guards to tease and play with, and endless servants who would bring you lovely things to eat or carry you on their shoulders. The little boy became a palace favourite and was allowed to go almost everywhere. So of course he poked his nose into everything.

His favourite places, besides the kitchens, were the workshops where all the things used in the palace were made. He liked to sit in the pottery which was wet and cool and smelled of clay, and watch the craftsmen turning big round water-pots, storage jars coiled like great snakes, and bowl after bowl all alike. They would give him a piece of clay and he would make it into a bird or a bowl or a fish, and then squish it up again and make something new.

From the pottery he liked to go to the metal-workers, and watch them pounding out ladles and trays and harness pieces and hinges and helmets and swords. In that shop he had to stay well out of the way, for it was full of fire and heavy hammers and banging and commotion. It was exciting but scary.

The carpenters' workshop, on the other hand, was a place to spend the whole day. Wood was rare in Egypt, and every piece was treasured. The carpenters made beautiful furniture and chests, wagons and wooden tools. When he was big enough they let him carve small pieces. They insisted that he finish what he began even if he cut his fingers, and he had to remember to put away his tools at the end. The carpenters, like all craftsmen, were careful of their tools and proud of their work.

Qulthum came with him sometimes. Her favourite place was the weavers' studio. The two children would sit on top of a big pile of cut flax or a soft bale of cotton, and watch the long shining stream of warp become cloth as the weaver sent the weft threads back and forth, back and forth. Moses often fell asleep there, with the sound of the regular movements of the shuttle matching his heart-beats: ka-thunk, ka-thunk.

Then there were the jewellers, and the leather workers, and the stone-masons, and...

But it was time for school. His chief teacher was the high priest himself, Haman, master of geometry, designer of pyramids, chief adviser to the Pharaoh.

Haman was the second most powerful person in the land, and everyone had to remember this all the time. When he walked, people bowed and got out of the way.

The first thing Haman taught Moses was to sit still. The second thing was to listen. The third was the names of the gods: Ra, the sun god, Isis, Osiris, Anubis – he took the boy to see their statues and described their powers and qualities.

"But why does Horus have the head of a falcon?" laughed Moses. "And why is Mut doing a backbend over the river?"

"Silly boy," said the priest, "The goddess Mut is the sky, bending over all of us. The goddess Hapi is the river, and without her rising and falling Egypt would not exist. There would be no flood to fertilize the fields with rich topsoil, and no end of the flood for planting and growing crops. Hapi is your mother. Don't forget it!"

Another mother. Moses already had two! For Asiya, the Pharaoh's wife, had quite taken to the child and spent time with him each day.

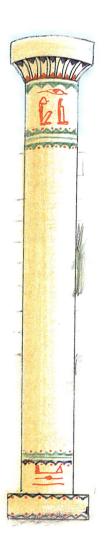

She taught him the songs and the language of Egypt. Often she listened to him, for although he was still young, he carried a kind of wisdom unknown to her. It came from his other mother, the one who lived outside.

From his other mother, Moses learned about the history of his true people. He learned how Abraham had destroyed the idols of his city, how he had been tied up and thrown into a fire, and had miraculously survived, completely unharmed. He learned about the two sons of Abraham, Isaac in Canaan and Ishmael in Arabia. He learned about Isaac's son Israel, for whom the whole Hebrew side of the family were named: Bani Israel, the Children of Israel. Again and again he asked for his favourite story, the tale of his great-great-many-greats grandfather, Joseph, and how he was tricked by his brothers and sold as a slave and brought to Egypt, where he became very powerful and famous. Joseph brought all his tribe to live with him in Egypt and they had been there ever since! Moses loved this story more than all the others.

Then Moses would go back again to the high priest and learn about the other gods. He became quite confused.

"M-M-Mother!" he said to his mother, "Is the high priest very wise?"

"Well," said his mother thoughtfully, "you might say he is very wise in some things and not so wise in other things."

"M-M-Mother!" he stammered to his mother (from an early age Moses had had difficulty in speaking fluently), "Why does the high priest believe in so many gods and we believe in only one? He says it's better to have many to take care of everything! And look at their statues and their temples and their celebrations! Surely you must be leaving out a f-f-few!"

But his mother said, "Listen to your heart, boy! Could there be ten Pharaohs to rule Egypt? They would all fight! Only one God, only one. That One saved your life and is training you for something great! Don't you ever, ever forget it!"

Moses took long walks in the palace gardens. He saw the growth and flowering of the plants, the fruits bursting with juice, the dates hanging in great bunches from the palms. He smelled and felt the air, the heat, the warmth of the good earth underfoot. He knew it was all one thing, and he a part of it. He was content; his mother was right. Then he found the papyrus.

The great reeds bobbed their heads over the river and he and Qulthum were playing hide and seek among them. He could not find her. He knew how still she could be. Looking carefully this way and that, he crept along, and suddenly bumped right into a stooping man! Moses jumped back, and the man jumped up, a curved knife in his hand! Qulthum screamed from behind them both, but the man only laughed.

"Watch where you're going, youngster. You wouldn't want to spoil the Pharaoh's papyrus, now would you?"

"Oh!" said Qulthum. "My brother told me about papyrus! He is teaching me how to write!"

"Oh ho!" said the man, laughing at her. "So you'll be the first little Hebrew girl to ever learn to write hieroglyphs! Whatever for?"

"Don't you t-t-tease her!" said Moses angrily. "She is very s-s-smart! What are you doing?"

"Well, your Highness, I'm cutting reeds, as you can plainly see!"

"Wh-Why?"

"To make papyrus. Come, I'll show you."

Off they went to a whole hidden workshop that Moses had never seen before. Many people were pounding the reeds and squashing them open on rocks. Then they soaked them in something and then they laid them one over the other.

"It's like weaving!" said Qulthum. "Like weaving, only the pieces stick together with some kind of glue...look! Someone is rolling them flat!"

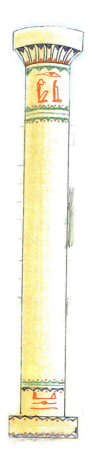
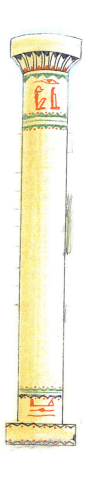

"Yes," said the man, "flat and dry and clean and ready for the scribes to write their writings. Beautiful, isn't it?"

Moses was looking at the straw-coloured pieces. He was very excited. All of a sudden he understood that the reeds growing out of the mud of the river were cut by human hands, and changed by human hands into something smooth and beautiful, and then written on in holy characters (hieroglyphs) to say the most important things about life and death and God and...

"Why is it called 'h-h-h-holy writing'?" he asked his teacher the next day, after he had been practising writing very hard for an hour.

"Because it is a gift from the gods, and is best used in the service of the gods," answered the teacher seriously. He shook his head in sorrow about his best student's speaking problem; but he was pleased to hear the boy asking real questions. He didn't know that by now every time he said 'gods', Moses was quietly saying 'God' under his breath.

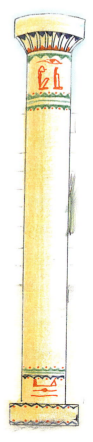

Chapter 3
A Terrible Night

So Moses grew up.

In the eyes of everyone in the palace and around about, in spite of not being an Egyptian, he was considered a prince. He could go anywhere, do anything (almost) and have what he wanted. He should have been a very happy young man. He was, except for one thing. He hated the way his Hebrew people were treated.

Although he had been trained to think as an Egyptian, he could not accept that the Hebrews were some kind of inferior race. Being one himself, he knew they were just like anyone else except for their belief in one God instead of many – and that was good, not bad. What did it matter if they had come from outside Egypt four hundred years earlier? Their first ancestor, Joseph, had been loved by the Pharaoh! And he gave them land, and invited them to stay! What was the problem? Anyhow many of them had married Egyptians, and they dressed and ate and looked like Egyptians. They had been there so long that most of them thought of themselves as Egyptians, yet everyone seemed to know the difference.

He knew that over time the Hebrews had become very rich and powerful, and because of this, the rulers of Egypt became fearful that the Hebrews would overpower them or unite with one of their foreign enemies. So they had decided to take away their rights and property – to make them slaves in fact.

When he saw the Children of Israel doing all the heavy dirty work, and being whipped and bossed about by Egyptians, he felt a great anger rising inside him. Moses had an in-built sense of justice. As he grew up he found that he could feel what was fair and what was unfair in his bones. Here was something unfair. What could he do?

Moses watched the Pharaoh and the high priest very carefully. He tried to work out how they governed Egypt. When he went to visit his mother, he would tell her, Qulthum and his brother, Aaron, all about the things he was learning. Aaron was older and had escaped being killed, but he had to be very careful of the Egyptians so he never came to visit the palace.

"Do you know what I did yesterday?" He said to Qulthum.

"Yes, I do. I saw you sitting in the great boat behind the Pharaoh, sailing down the Nile. There were a lot of fans waving, and everybody looked very serious. We had fun cheering from the banks and I waved at you. Did you see me?"

"N-No, I couldn't see you because I was busy looking serious. You know the the Pharaoh had a wig on and that heavy hat he wears and he had to hold the symbols of power, the shepherd's crook and the fan? Underneath the makeup and costume he looks bored. As long as he keeps up the act, the people are satisfied that their Pharaoh is doing his job."

"What is his job really?" asked Aaron.

"W-W-What's his job? Just to be the Pharaoh. The people think he's a g-g-god. They like to see him. Egypt basically rules itself. It runs by Nile time, river high, rest, river low, plant. You know that. But the Pharaoh can do whatever he wants because he's a god. They think he can do anything, make the sun rise, make the flood happen, anything. If he's careful to be there when the things happen anyway, the people think he's doing them. So he goes

out on the first day of the flood and they thank him for the flood. He prays to the sun and they think he's a son of the sun. G-G-Get it?"

But Moses knew from experience that behind the disguise, the real Pharaoh had to keep a firm hand on his nobles and priests, and he had to be careful that none of them got too strong. He also kept up the army and the palace police, and paid the generals well.

Another day he went to the temple of Ra, the sun god, and watched the other priests bow and scrape when Haman walked proudly by. But he knew from experience that those same priests all wanted to be the high priest themselves. Haman had to keep them in order like schoolboys. With all this watching and learning, Moses

knew a lot of things by the time he was a young man. But he still wanted to learn more. He always wanted to learn more. He was wiser than most young men and he could tell right from wrong, but he still had a problem with his temper, and he still couldn't work out what to do about his people, the Hebrews.

One day he left the palace and walked into the city to see what was going on. It was the hot time of day when most people were resting in their houses and not paying attention to what was going on in the streets. He came around a corner and there were two men having a fight. One of them was an Egyptian and one was a Hebrew. They were hitting and punching and yelling, and the Hebrew saw Moses and called to him for help.

All Moses' worries about his Hebrew people and all his sense of the injustices they lived with came rushing to the surface. He was furious. He rushed into the fight, and slugged the Egyptian hard. Too hard. Not only did he knock him down, he killed him.

There was silence. Moses stood looking at the fallen Egyptian, and the other man, who was a coward, ran away. Moses thought, "My temper is from the devil! And he will do anything to make me hurt myself! Look what I have done!"

He prayed hard for forgiveness and he said to God, "Oh You Who have always given me everything! I vow by all the blessings you have given me, I will never again help people who are bad people." For he realized that although the man was a Hebrew, he was not a good man. All Hebrews are not good and all Egyptians are not bad. That was the lesson he got from that. He went home, scared.

The next morning he felt he had to go back to the city again, and he was looking fearfully about when, what should happen? The very same man who called to him the day before called out for help again! Once again he was having a fight with an Egyptian.

Moses said to him, "Look here, you, you are clearly a troublemaker and it's your own fault!" Even so, forgetting his vow of the day before, he went to help him, but before he could do anything, the Egyptian he was fighting said, "Oh Moses, do you intend to kill me the way you killed another man yesterday? Your only aim is to become a bully and a tyrant, and you don't care to be a fair person!"

And right then a man came running, running from the far end of the city, and he cried out to Moses, all out of breath, "Oh Moses! Listen! The officials and priests are meeting right now to discuss you and they intend to kill you! You know they've always been jealous of you! Get out of here, quickly, quickly, I am one of those who wish you well!"

Without wasting a second, Moses ran. He ran through back alleys and side streets and took the paths he and Qulthum had explored as children. He got quickly away from the city and raced fearfully through the farms and reached the desert.

He prayed continuously for help, for he was going into the wilderness, and into the desert and its waterless wastes. Taking one last look back at the green banks of the Nile and the places of his childhood, he turned his face towards Madyan, the strange and unknown land of rock and sand where only the shepherds lived.

Moses began to walk more slowly, and as he caught his breath he thought. "Probably God has done all this to lead me to something right and good. These people out here (please God protect me from the bad ones) are Arabs, and they are a lot like the Hebrews. We have the same ancestors, the two sons of Abraham. They are more like me than the Egyptians. I can almost understand their language. Maybe they are not so wild as everyone thinks. Perhaps they will help me – I hope so, for indeed, I need it."

CHAPTER 4
THE DESERT

Two girls were waiting near a well in the middle of the Desert of Madyan. They had been there for several hours already, and they knew that they would have to wait some more. There were many flocks of sheep and goats there that day, and the rough men who led them were not interested in giving the girls a turn. They were too shy to push their way into the crowd, and they had no man to help them. So they waited, hot and dusty, with all their thirsty bleating sheep.

Then they saw a man walking out of the desert. He had no herd, and no bags, and no camel. What was he doing there? They saw him pause, and lean against a palm tree, and watch. Then, oddly, he came towards them. They were nervous. They did not know what to say to a strange man.

He came right up to them and asked, "What's the matter with you?"

"You tell him!" whispered one to the other.

"No, you tell him!" whispered the other to the first one. So they both said:

"We cannot water our animals until the herdsmen drive their animals home, for we are alone and weak, and our father is a very old man!"

"That's not fair," said the stranger. "Let me help you." Before they could say anything, he had called the leader of the sheep and the whole flock followed to the well. After he had watered them and brought them back, Moses went to sit under a tree in the shade and prayed. "Oh God!

Please, I need any good you can give me right now!" He had no food, no place to go, and no family.

The two girls took their sheep and went home, but they talked all the way about the kind stranger. When they got to their tent, they told their father what had happened. He listened carefully and then said, "Go right back and invite him to eat with us. Such a good man should be rewarded."

One of the girls returned and found Moses still resting under the tree. She came towards him shyly, and said in a quiet voice, "My father invites you to our tent, so he can reward you for having watered our flock for us!"

So Moses went and met the girls' father, and ate a good meal which they had cooked with great care. Then they talked. Their father asked Moses all about himself, and Moses told him the story of his life. It was late when at last he finished. One of the daughters whispered to her father, "O father! Hire him to work with us! He is very strong and we trust him!"

He smiled at his daughter. This possibility had been in his mind from the beginning. He gazed at Moses kindly and said, "Consider this. You are alone and have no family and no money and no flocks. We are in need of help. I am willing to let you marry one of these two daughters of mine, if you will remain with us for eight years of service. If you would stay for ten years, that would be generous of you. But I don't want to ask too much of you, I want to be fair."

Moses agreed to this idea immediately. He liked the girls, he liked their father, and he had absolutely no other place on earth to go.

As the fire burned low and the stars turned overhead, the girls' father, known as Shu'ayb, spoke again. "The real truth is that God has guided you to me. I am a descendant of your beloved Joseph and his father Jacob and his grandfather Abraham, for I too am a prophet. God has

brought you out of Egypt and sent you to me to complete your instruction to be a prophet, for you are not just to be a shepherd. You are safe here. Welcome."

So Moses stayed. All his princely education had never taught him much about sheep, but he was strong and clear with them and they followed him willingly. His upbringing had given him the air of command and authority, and soon all the other herdsmen got out of the way when he brought Shu'ayb's flocks to water. He married one of the girls, and they had two sons, and the sheep had lambs, and the lambs grew, and life went on.

He learned much from his prophetic father-in-law. The knowledge was similar to what his mother had taught him, but it was more profound, and he found his understanding growing day by day. He learned to control his temper. He could see the true character of the people he met, as if he could read their hearts and minds. The desert emptied his brain of all the difficulties of his childhood, and he felt strong and clear.

When the grass ran out in one place, they moved to another. They rolled up the tents and put all their bags on the camels and went somewhere else. It happened that one night, (because it was too hot to travel in the day), they were wandering in the desert looking for new pastures. They were moving through an awesome landscape of desert and wind-carved stone, when Moses saw a light in the distance. It seemed to be a fire; it was on the slope of the mountain they called Sinai.

He said to his family, "Wait here! Look, I see a fire far away over there. Perhaps I can bring you some news from the people there, or at least I can get a burning branch from the fire, so you might warm yourselves!"

Off he went into the night and began climbing up the slopes of the mountain until he came to a small valley, where he saw the source of the light. Over to his right was a low tree, which seemed to be burning, but actually it was simply filled with a glowing, heavenly light. And then he heard the Voice:

"Blessed are all who are near this fire!

"O Moses! Truly, I am God, the Almighty, the Wise, the Sustainer of all the worlds!"

Moses began to shiver, and his hair stood on end. He looked all around to find the source of the Voice, but all he could see was the light.

The Voice spoke again: "Take off your sandals! You are in the sacred Valley of Tuwa, and I have chosen you to be My messenger! Listen!

"I, I alone, am God, there are no other gods besides Me. So worship only Me, and remember Me in your prayers! Never listen to people who only follow their own whims and wishes. Follow My revelations, O Moses, for at the end of time everyone will be rewarded for what they did in this life. Now, what is this in your right hand?"

Somehow Moses found the strength to answer: "It is my s-s-staff, I lean on it, and I beat down leaves for my s-s-sheep with it, and I use it for a lot of things." In his awe Moses' stammer, which he thought had almost disappeared, returned.

God said: "Throw it down, Moses!"

Moses threw it down, but oh! It turned into a snake, coiling and uncoiling right at his feet! Moses jumped back, but the Voice said,

"Do not be afraid! My chosen ones do not have to be afraid of anything! Take hold of it, pick it up, and I shall make it a staff again!"

Moses grabbed the snake, and there in his hand was his old familiar staff. Things were happening very fast. God spoke again:

"Now put your right hand close to your chest. Now take it out."

Moses' hand, dark brown from the sun and scarred from work, came out pure white, without a mark or blemish, shining with light like the bush!

"Do not ever be afraid again. You are safe in this world and the next! These shall be the two signs you will take to the Pharaoh and his nobles. They do not worship Me, they worship many gods, and you are to go to them and make them set free the Children of Israel, the tribe of your family and your ancestors!"

But Moses was quick to see a number of problems in this command. So he replied, "O my God! I have k-k-killed one of them, so I fear they will kill me! P-p-please protect me from them, and open my heart to Your light, and make my job easy for me! Loosen this knot from my t-t-tongue so they may fully understand my speech! And my speech is so slow. Let me find my brother, Aaron – he is a far better speaker than I – to help me and stand with me and explain what I say!"

God said: "I shall strengthen you through your brother, and give you both power, and they will not be able to touch you. You both will carry My messages, and you and all who follow you shall be successful! I have been looking after you all this time? Remember, "I inspired your mother in a dream, saying, 'Place him in a basket and throw it into the river, and the river will cast him ashore, and one who is an enemy to Me and an enemy to him will adopt him.'

"That is how early I spread My love over you, so you might be trained and formed under My guidance and protection!

"And I was there when your sister went out and said to the Pharaoh's people, 'Shall I guide you to a woman who might take charge of him?' So I returned you to your mother, so her eyes might be happy instead of full of tears, and she would not sorrow any more!

"And when you grew up, you killed a man, but I forgave you and saved you from them, although I gave you other trials. Nobody who has done wrong and then replaced the wrong with some good needs to fear Me. Then you stayed for years among the people of Madyan, and now you have come here as I ordered, for I have chosen you for My Own service.

"Now go, you and your brother, spread My words, and do not forget Me or get tired of remembering Me! Go to those misguided people who do not worship Me. But speak to the Pharaoh in a mild manner, so he has a chance to remember himself, or at least to feel fear!

"Do not worry about what he might do! He cannot touch you! I shall be with you both, hearing and seeing all. Now go, for the Pharaoh has gone too far. Tell him: 'We bear a message from the Sustainer of all the worlds: Let the Children of Israel go with us!'"

CHAPTER 5
BACK TO EGYPT

Moses took his family back to Egypt. He and Aaron went to see the Pharaoh straightaway.

The Pharaoh was a very strong man and was often busy building pyramids and statues and temples all over Egypt. Beside him stood his old minister, Haman, who knew Moses well. The Pharaoh looked down from his throne at these two Hebrew visitors and frowned. He spoke:

"Didn't we bring you up among us when you were a child? And didn't you spend years of your life with us? Yet even so, you did that terrible thing, you killed an Egyptian, and have shown that you are ungrateful! Now you are back. Why?"

Moses was ready for this. He replied, "I committed that crime while I was still young and ignorant, and I ran away from you because I feared you. But since then, my God has given me the ability to judge between right and wrong, and has made me one of His messengers. As for any favours I have received from you: I would not have needed them if you had not enslaved my people!"

"I see," said the Pharaoh. "And what do you want this time?"

"My brother and I have come as messengers from God, the Sustainer of all the worlds, and He tells you to let the Children of Israel go with us, and not to make them suffer any more. You will not have any peace until you do that. Also you should stop worshipping other gods, and worship the One God, Who gives you life! Otherwise, in the life to come, you will suffer terribly, and in this world you will never be satisfied!"

Said the Pharaoh, with a slight tight smile, "And what - or who - is this 'Sustainer of all the worlds'?"

Moses answered, "He is the One Who created and sustains the heavens and the earth and all that is between them, and who one day will destroy them and create them again!"

The Pharaoh opened his eyes wide and looked around the splendid room at his courtiers and nobles and priests, and said, "Did you hear that?"

All the courtiers and nobles and priests nodded their heads and smiled and tittered a little.

But Moses did not give up. "He is your Sustainer too, not just mine, and the Sustainer of your forefathers and of everyone and everything! There is NO other power equal to Him!"

The Pharaoh looked at the people and said, "Behold, this 'messenger' who claims that he has been sent to you is mad! His words are eloquent, but we certainly do NOT believe him!"

Moses was patient. "He is God of the East and the West and everywhere in between. He made all of Nature for you, and gave you the means to live, and sends down the rain so the plants can grow. We eat, and we pasture cattle. He created us out of this earth, and puts us back into it, and will bring us out of it again! If you desire purity and real knowledge, I can teach you all these things, but if you do not, you are doomed!"

The Pharaoh heard and understood; but he was too proud, and he refused to pay attention.

He said, "Oh you nobles! I did not know that you could have any god other than myself! Well, then, O Haman, kindle me a fire to bake some clay bricks, and then build me a high tower, so I can climb up and

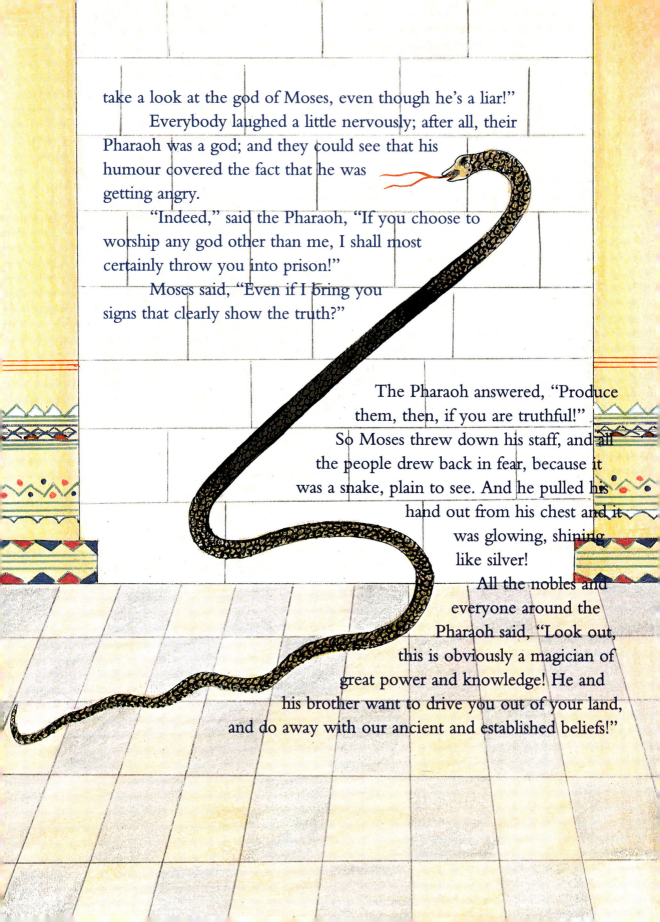

take a look at the god of Moses, even though he's a liar!"

Everybody laughed a little nervously; after all, their Pharaoh was a god; and they could see that his humour covered the fact that he was getting angry.

"Indeed," said the Pharaoh, "If you choose to worship any god other than me, I shall most certainly throw you into prison!"

Moses said, "Even if I bring you signs that clearly show the truth?"

The Pharaoh answered, "Produce them, then, if you are truthful!"

So Moses threw down his staff, and all the people drew back in fear, because it was a snake, plain to see. And he pulled his hand out from his chest and it was glowing, shining like silver!

All the nobles and everyone around the Pharaoh said, "Look out, this is obviously a magician of great power and knowledge! He and his brother want to drive you out of your land, and do away with our ancient and established beliefs!"

The Pharaoh agreed. He said to them, "What do you advise?" They answered, "The priests of Amon are wise in the ways of magic. Let him and his brother wait awhile, and send heralds to all the cities to collect all the sorcerers of great knowledge. They will defeat him and win a great victory for you and the other gods!"

The Pharaoh turned to Moses. He was no longer smiling. "Have you come to drive us out of our land by your sorcery, Moses? Have you come to force us out of the religion of our forefathers? We can certainly produce the same magic as you. Set a date," he said, "for our contest and a suitable place. We will be there – see that you are also!"

"The day of the great festival," said Moses, "by the river, when the sun has risen high."

So the Pharaoh and his priests and nobles sent for the sorcerers, and plotted and planned and schemed about the best way to defeat Moses. The sorcerers were assembled at a set time on the feast day, and the people were asked, "Are you all here, so we may have a great procession behind the sorcerers when they defeat Moses?"

"We are here!" shouted the people. They were very excited. They all accepted magic as a part of life, a part of their religion. Never before had so many magicians and important people been gathered in one place!

On a raised platform over the river the magicians stood in front of the Pharaoh and bowed low. They said, "We should have a great reward if we win!"

The Pharaoh answered, "Yes, and when you win you will indeed be among those who are close to me! Now go out there all together, united, and defeat this liar who wants to deny our ancient beliefs!" Satisfied, the magicians looked at Moses, who was standing with his brother a little to one side.

"Shall we throw first or will you throw?" they asked.

"You go ahead and throw whatever you are going to throw!" said Moses.

So the magicians of Egypt threw their magic ropes and their magic staffs, and they were so clever that they made it seem to the audience that the staffs actually wriggled and writhed and were really live snakes.

In his heart, Moses was worried. God said to him: "Do not be afraid! You shall win! Now throw that staff which is in your right hand - it will swallow up all of theirs, for they have made only a magician's artful fake, and the magician can never do any good, however much he may try to!"

The magicians were pleased with themselves, and said, "By the Pharaoh's might, look, we have won!"

But they spoke too soon. Moses threw his staff - and it became a snake - and it ate up their ropes and staffs, one after the other until they were all gone. The people were looking at an empty space where those

wriggling things had been. Moses calmly bent over and picked up his snake, which became a staff again at his touch. All the magicians' tools were inside it!

Immediately the sorcerers sank down on their knees, prostrating themselves on the ground, and exclaiming, "We have come to believe in the Sustainer of all the worlds, the God of Moses and Aaron!"

The Pharaoh was furious. "Have you believed in him before I have given you permission? Moses is now your master, is he? You shall know my revenge! I shall cut off your hands and your feet because of your denial of me, and I shall crucify you in great numbers, all together, on the trunks of palm trees! I'm going to do this so you will know for certain which of us can inflict a more severe punishment and which is more powerful, his god or ME!"

But the magicians answered, "You cannot harm us." They knew that what they had witnessed was not magic but a sign from God.

The Pharaoh rose. "This is clearly only sorcery. Leave me to kill Moses - and then let him call upon his little god! I fear he will influence my people and steer them away from worshipping me and our other gods, towards his god; he will do nothing but cause disturbance and corruption in the country!"

Moses answered, "I do not fear you, Oh Pharaoh, I am safe under the protection of the One True God."

Chapter 6
TRIALS

The Pharaoh and his priests were naturally very put out by the results of the contest. They remained convinced that Moses was nothing but a skilful magician. "He is nothing but a caster of spells, a liar!" they said. So when Moses and Aaron came again to see him, the Pharaoh was not in a good mood.

"All this talk of God is something you have cleverly made up," said the Pharaoh. "We have never heard anything like it before so it cannot be true. I am god here. You are very eloquent, and Moses is a clever magician, but as to your request: no."

Moses answered, "God knows best. He will send other signs, and perhaps you will be c-c-convinced. I warn you, one last time, you should listen to Him!"

But the priests said to Moses, "Whatever sign you may produce before us, in order to cast a spell on us, we shall not believe you!" And they said to each other, "How can we believe them - two mortals like ourselves - and their people are our slaves?"

Then there began the series of plagues.

First there was a drought. The flood came late and scarcely at all, and the crops dried up. That is, the Egyptians' crops dried up. The Hebrew crops seemed to thrive.

The next year, the Nile flooded and washed away houses and cattle and everything in its path. Everything, that is, except the small huts and houses of the Children of Israel.

Then after that, just as the wheat was growing ripe, there came another plague – this time swarms and swarms of locusts. They flew down on the crops and gobbled them all up and only straw was left in the fields.

Then the Pharaoh's people came to Moses, and said, "O Moses, pray for us to your god, because you have a connection with him. If you remove this plague from us, we will truly believe in you, and we promise we will let the Children of Israel go with you!"

So Moses prayed, and God removed the locusts. Then he went before the Pharaoh and said, "Well?"

The Pharaoh looked at him coldly and said,

"The locusts always go away. You and your 'god' did not have anything to do with it. Egypt has always had blessings without you. Go away!"

Two minutes later the Pharaoh began to scratch, because the next plague was lice! They crawled all over everybody – everybody that is except the Children of Israel, of course. When the whole palace nearly came to a standstill because of the itching, the nobles came to Moses again. "Oh Moses, pray for us to your god, because you are connected to him. If you remove this plague from us, we will truly believe in you, and will let the Children of Israel go with you!"

So Moses prayed, and God removed the lice. Then he went to the Pharaoh and said, "Well?"

"Well what?" said the Pharaoh. "Of course the lice went away. They have been known to come from time to time. Not so many, perhaps, but they have come before. It's the hot weather. Go away!"

The next time the Pharaoh lifted his wine goblet to drink, there was a frog in it! He dropped it with a crash, and shouted for the butler and the maid and the cook and the wine steward. They all came running at once, but they never reached the the Pharaoh, because they tripped and slipped and stepped on the frogs that were hopping all over the floor. Nobody could sleep without checking their bed first and throwing out the frogs. Nobody could hear anybody else because of their very loud croaking. When the Pharaoh couldn't get any dinner because the food was spoiled by frogs and nobody could hear him yelling, he sent for Moses himself.

"O Moses, pray for us to your god, because you have a connection with him. If you remove this plague from us, we will truly believe in you, and I promise I will let the Children of Israel go with you!"

So Moses prayed, and God removed the frogs. Then he said, "Well?"

"Well what?" said the Pharaoh. "Of course the frogs went away. The great cranes and egrets ate them up. Those birds are worthy of worship, not your imaginary god! Go away!" And he put more pressures on the Children of Israel and gave them even more work to do, to prove he had the most power in Egypt.

But the next time the Pharaoh wanted a drink of water, the water was red, and looked and smelled suspiciously like blood. The people were terrified because the Nile was red, and there was nothing to drink. In their fear and terror they asked Moses to pray again. Moses was becoming a very, very patient man. So he prayed again.

The blood went away. Moses went before the Pharaoh and said, "Well?"

"Well what?" sneered the Pharaoh. "There was never any blood. That was just some of your magic, and I'm getting tired of it!" He sent out criers to all the parts of his kingdom with this message:

"O my people! Doesn't the power over Egypt belong to me, since all the clear running waters flow at my feet? Can't you see that I am your supreme lord? Am I, your Pharaoh, not better than this worthless man who can hardly make his meaning clear? If he's so great, why hasn't he been given royal golden armlets? Why have no angels been sent with him?"

The people laughed, and obeyed their Pharaoh, for they didn't want to believe in anything else. All but a few of them, who had become followers of Moses and listened to him. One of these was his foster-mother, 'Asiya, the Pharaoh's wife.

She had been in great distress as she watched her husband puff himself up, increase his persecutions and harden his heart against all she knew to be true. She had no one to turn to but God, and she prayed:

"O my Lord! Build for me, near to Yourself, a mansion in the Garden, and save me from the Pharaoh and his doings, and save me from those who do wrong!"

God spoke again to Moses. Moses went to his sister, and his brother, and the people who had stood by him through all these difficulties. He asked Aaron to convey this message: "God has tried the Egyptians with many trials and given them many chances to listen and believe. Yet the Pharaoh just keeps breaking his promises. You see how it is. Now God is telling us to prepare to leave. Go out and tell all the Children of Israel to sacrifice a lamb for each house. Then they should smear some blood of the lamb over their doorways, and go inside and stay inside! And they should make bread without yeast, because there isn't time for it to rise, and they should pack their belongings and be ready to flee. And do not be afraid!"

That night the Angel of Death moved through Egypt. Death struck the first-born of every family, of people and of animals, every one, but he passed over the houses where the door was smeared with the blood of the sacrifice. In the middle of the night a great cry arose in Egypt, because not one family was left untouched by pain and sorrow. And Moses prepared himself, and led his people out of their houses, and they fled.

They took with them everything that could walk or that they could carry on their backs and the backs of their donkeys and camels and cows. They took their flocks and their stored food and their clothes and their jewels. They bundled up their babies and old folks and the strong carried the weak. Off they went, and they had with them a very important casket. In it was the mummy of Joseph. Some four hundred years before, he had said to the people, "God will surely visit you, and you shall carry up my bones away from here with you!" And the people remembered.

Chapter 7
THE EXODUS

Moses knew they would be pursued. God had warned him. He strode along at the head of the great crowd of his people, and remembered God's orders: "Go forth with My servants by night, and strike out for them a dry path through the sea; fear not of being overtaken, and do not dread the sea!" So, rather than take the obvious northern route, they moved out across the wilderness towards the Red Sea. The people didn't understand. They were complaining and shaking their heads already. The Pharaoh's army was sure to follow, and they had chariots and fast horses. Moses marched on.

There appeared in front of him, out of nowhere, a pillar of fire. Moses felt his skin prickle, as it had by the bush in the Valley of Tuwa. He followed the fire. After a while they rested, then rose again, and went on. By day the pillar of fire became a pillar of smoke.

The people moved, but painfully slowly, because of their things and their young and their old. They were constantly looking back to see if the Pharaoh's army was coming. Still they saw no one.

Meanwhile the Pharaoh was told that the Children of Israel had fled. He rose up in great anger, and said, "What have we done, to let them go? They are just a weak and worthless band, but they hate us because they see what we are. They see we are a nation united and prepared for

anything! In the past they thought they could live like us, but we have rightly driven them out of their gardens and springs, and taken away their money and their high positions and made them our servants!

"Now they are running away! Call out the guard, call up the army, prepare the chariots! We will capture them and show them who has the last word in Egypt!"

A great army gathered and streamed out across the desert. The path of the moving Hebrews was easy to follow. Soon they saw, catching the morning light, the great cloud of dust raised by the many thousands of hooves and feet. And beyond it, they saw the sea.

At the same time, those at the back of the fleeing Hebrews saw the sun glinting on the armour and the shields of the Pharaoh's army. They set up a great cry. Some began to pray, and others shouted to Moses, "Because there were no graves in Egypt, have you brought us out here to die in the wilderness? How have you done this to us? Didn't we tell you in Egypt, 'Leave us alone, so we can serve the Egyptians? Didn't we tell you? It would have been better for us to serve the Egyptians than die in the desert!"

And others cried out, looking fearfully from the army to the sea, "Where can we go? We shall surely be overtaken and defeated!"

But Moses said calmly, "No! God is with me, and He will guide me! Stand still and watch how your Lord saves you." And he struck the water with his staff.

A kind of stillness came over the hosts of tired people, eager horses, fierce warriors. Time seemed to stop. There came a hissing and a roaring from the sea, a strong east wind arose, and the waters began to pull apart. Two great mountainous waves formed on either side of the spot where Moses had struck his staff.

As the water pulled up and away, fishes, crabs, octopi, and squid flopped and flipped on the wet sand, trying to get back into their own environment.

The army recovered its wits, and began to advance. "Move!" shouted Moses, and confidently strode out on the road between the walls of water.

The people had no choice. Those who didn't believe had to believe now. Facing what seemed like certain death in both directions, they followed Moses. They hurried. They urged on the slowest, they carried the lame, they left what held them back and they ran. They got across and felt dry land under their feet and turned to look back.

There, entering between the mountains of water, was the Pharaoh at the head of his great army. Still completely full of self-importance, he must have believed that the water had separated for him. He stood in the lead chariot and shouted defiantly to the Hebrews, to Moses, to God. As he reached the centre of the sea, with all his army close behind him, the walls of water fell.

About to drown, the Pharaoh screamed, "At last I believe there is no god except the God the Children of Israel believe in, and I surrender myself to Him!!!"

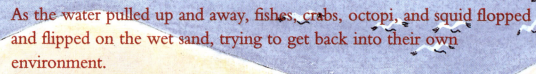

He heard God answer, "Now? When before you always rebelled against Me, and spread lies? You acted as if you would never come before Me and be judged for what you did! Today I shall save only your body, to be an example to those who will come after you! As for you, you are a thing of the past. You are cursed in this world and the next!" Then the Pharaoh, Haman, the generals, and all the army were buried in the sea and drowned. And that was the end of them. Everything they had done and everything they had built was utterly destroyed. The Pharaoh's body floated to the surface and was found, and made into a mummy, and can be seen to this day, an example for others.★

The Hebrews sat down and caught their breath. Some prayed, some wept. All of them were utterly amazed. After a while they got up and moved again. Moses led his people on, out of the darkness into the light, and as long as they followed him, they prospered. They had many, many adventures during their time in the desert – but these make up another story.

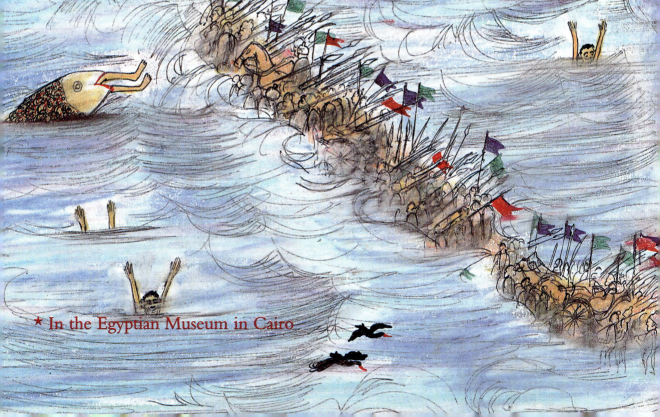

★ In the Egyptian Museum in Cairo.

The LIVES OF THE PROPHETS Series

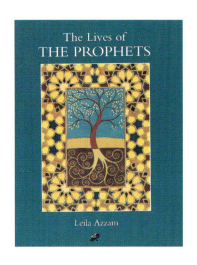
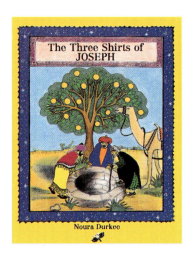